My First Words and Pictures

Brita Granström

WALKER BOOKS

AND SUBSIDIARIES

My name is Sam and this is my family.

Sam Ted   Mum   Dad Bobby Molly   Oscar

This is my house.

This is my bedroom. It's blue, red and yellow.

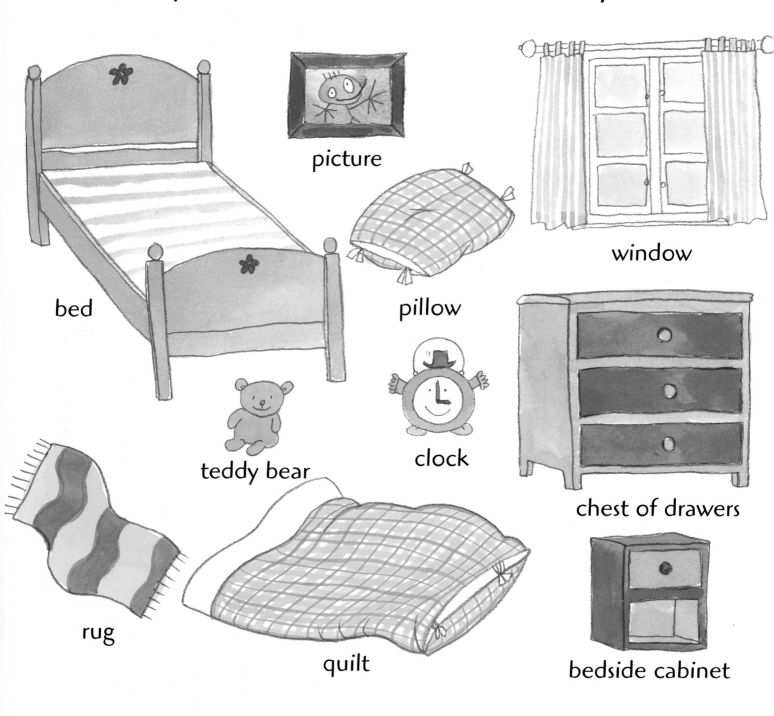

picture

window

bed

pillow

teddy bear

clock

chest of drawers

rug

quilt

bedside cabinet

And these are some of my favourite clothes.

vest

cardigan

pants

socks

dress

jumper

trainers

dungarees

What shall I wear today?

shorts

T-shirt

hat

coat

sandals

boots

gloves

party dress

scarf

shoes

In the morning we have breakfast together in the kitchen.

table

egg

cereal

cup

bowl

bread

bottle

butter

jam

bib

plate

milk

highchair

Then I go to playschool.

ride

paint

dance

build

Look at all the fun things we do!

sing

cuddle

skip

jump

crawl

wave

Some mornings we go to the park.

swing

slide

bench

bin

duck

pigeon

tree

ball

pushchair

When I come home I'm hungry.
These are all my favourite foods.

sandwich

tomato

cheese

yoghurt

orange

biscuits

apple

carrot

honey

juice

banana

grapes

I love to play in the garden with Oscar.
Look at all the things in our garden.

flowerpot

butterfly

ladybird

bee

flower

caterpillar   snail

watering-can

Bobby and I love to play with all our toys!

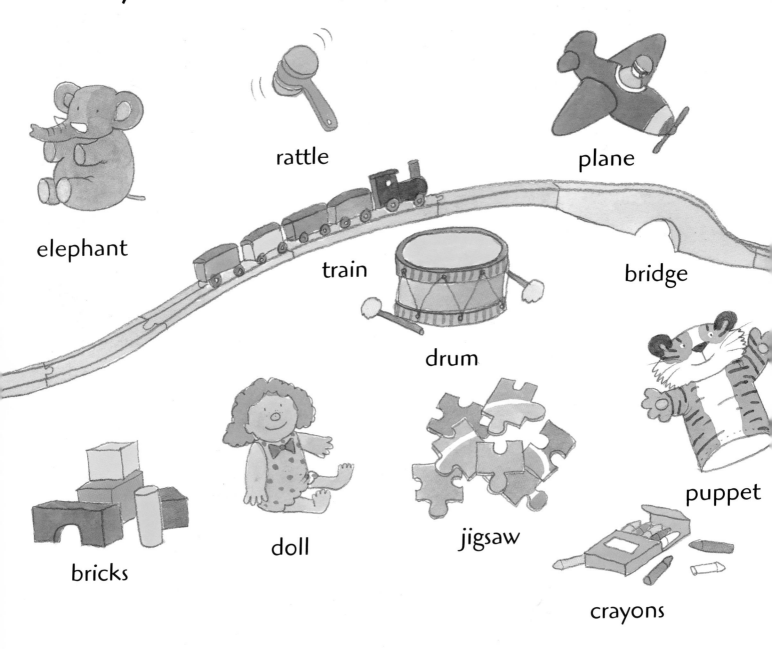

rattle

plane

elephant

train

bridge

drum

bricks

doll

jigsaw

puppet

crayons

Some days we all go out in the car.

car

bicycle

motor bike

lorry

bus

ambulance

digger

Sometimes we visit Gran and Grandad on the farm.

scarecrow

pig

chicks

hen

goat

tractor

horse   sheep   cockerel   cow

And, on sunny days, we go to the beach.

sandcastle

bucket

spade

sun block

swimsuit

towel

beach umbrella

sunhat

sunglasses

ice-cream

sun

crab

shells

Today it's my birthday. I'm having a party with balloons and a big cake.

badge

card

balloons

party hats

present

pizza

lemonade

candles

crisps

birthday cake

popcorn

Bobby and I always have a bath with
lots of bubbles before we go to bed ...

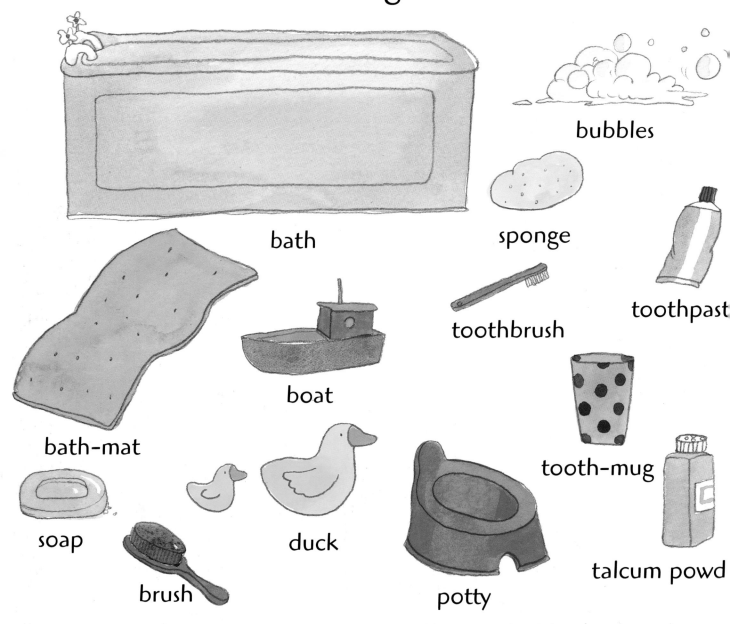

bath

bubbles

sponge

toothpast

bath-mat

boat

toothbrush

tooth-mug

soap

brush

duck

potty

talcum powd

and, best of all, a bedtime story.
Goodnight!

moon

stars

lamp

slippers

dummy

sofa

pyjamas

book

dressing-gown

For Lill-Lisa with love

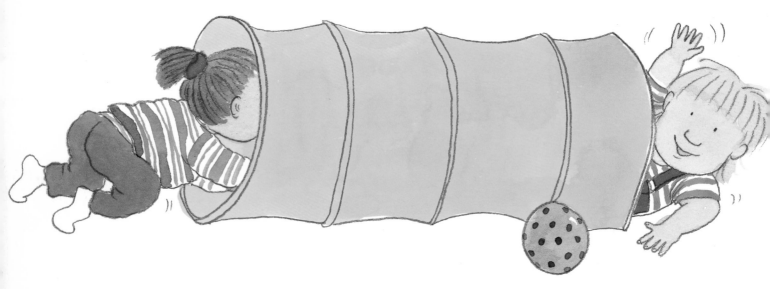

First published 1998 by Walker Books Ltd
87 Vauxhall Walk, London SE11 5HJ

This edition published 2004

2 4 6 8 10 9 7 5 3 1

© 1998 Brita Granström

This book has been typeset in Highlander

Printed in China

British Library Cataloguing in Publication Data:
a catalogue record for this book is available from the British Library

ISBN 1-84428-452-2